D0550169

BALNAIN PRIMARY SCHOOL
GLENURQUHART
INVERNESS
IV3 6TJ

Shot down

R.I.C. Publications® Pty Ltd

ASTONISHING HEADLINES

Attacked	Missing
Captured	**Shot down**
Condemned	Stowed away
Kidnapped	Stranded at sea
Lost and found	Trapped

First published SADDLEBACK PUBLISHING, INC.
Three Watson Irvine, CA 92618-2767

Published under licence 2006 by R.I.C. PUBLICATIONS® PTY LTD
PO Box 332 Greenwood 6924 Western Australia
www.ricgroup.com.au

Distributed by:
Australasia
R.I.C. Publications, PO Box 332, Greenwood 6924, Western
Australia:
www.ricgroup.com.au

United Kingdom and Republic of Ireland
Prim-Ed Publishing, Bosheen, New Ross, Co. Wexford, Ireland:
www.prim-ed.com

Asia
R.I.C. Publications, 5th Floor, Gotanda Mikado Building,
2-5-8 Hiratsuka, Shinagawa-Ku Tokyo, Japan 142-0051:
www.ricpublications.com

Photo credits: cover, AFP/Getty Images; page 28, Joe Bela, Getty;
page 29, Copley News Service; page 57, C.E. Mitchell, BlackStar
Photos

ISBN10   1-74126-516-9
ISBN13   978-1-74126-516-3

Printed in Singapore

CONTENTS

Introduction

It is every pilot's nightmare: getting hit by a missile or enemy bullets.

The attack usually comes from behind. An enemy fighter follows the plane, comes in close and then shoots.

Sometimes the attack is a missile shot from the ground. Sometimes it is anti-aircraft fire.

Maybe the plane explodes. Maybe it just loses an engine. Maybe the pilot cannot control the plane. The plane is no longer a flying machine. It is a huge piece of metal falling to Earth. Just a little damage can cause any plane to crash.

But the pilot and crew can bail out of a warplane if it starts to go down. If the crew is lucky and quick, they will float to the earth by parachute.

Nobody can bail out of a passenger plane. If a missile hits, it usually crashes, killing everyone on board.

Fighter pilots around the world have an agreement. They do not shoot down passenger planes. They only attack other warplanes.

However these rules are not always followed. Sometimes accidents do happen. In this book, you will read about planes that were shot down. Some were warplanes in times of war. Some were passenger planes in times of peace. Sometimes the people on board survived.

Sometimes they did not survive.

DATAFILE

TIME LINE ▶▶▶▶

December 1941

> The United States of America declares war on Germany.

March 1944

> Chuck Yeager's fighter plane is shot down over Bordeaux, France.

Where is Bordeaux?

KEY TERMS ▶▶▶▶

altitude	the vertical position of an object above the sea or land
elevator	part of the small wing at the back of a plane used to make the plane go up or down
rudder	the part of a plane or boat used to steer it
cockpit	the front of the plane where the pilot sits and controls the plane

Chapter 1

Ace pilot shot down

On 5 March 1944, Chuck Yeager took off from England. His P-51 fighter plane and three others, headed for Bordeaux, France.

Below them, World War II raged. The German army had taken over France. Yeager's mission: To find German bombers at secret airfields in France and destroy them.

A dangerous mission

German fighter planes protected the airfields. They patrolled the skies, looking for British and American planes.

Yeager and the others flew in a diamond-shaped formation. Yeager flew in the rear–the most dangerous position. The German pilots usually attacked the back plane first.

Yeager had a lot to watch out for. He had to stay with the other planes. He had to look for bombers on the ground, and for enemy fighter planes in the air. He also had to watch his plane's instruments and controls.

Hunting planes

Yeager was a good pilot—quick, alert, brave and smart. He had grown up in the mountains of West Virginia in the United States of America. He knew how to hunt. But now he was not hunting rabbits and squirrels. He was hunting enemy planes.

He was good at it. Yeager had already shot down two planes, and he had always flown home safely. But Yeager's luck was about to run out.

German fighter planes

Three German FW-190 fighters came swooping in from behind. Yeager saw the tracer bullet trails zip past his plane. He tried to dodge them, but it was too late.

As the bullets hit his plane, they cut its elevator cables. Yeager could not control the elevator wing at the back of the plane. He could not change his altitude.

To get away, Yeager used his rudder to do a snap roll. As the plane rolled to the side and spun upside down, the blood rushed to his head. Yeager escaped the attack, but he knew he would crash.

'I just got hit.'

Pilots do not like to bail out of their planes. It is never easy and always dangerous. There is little time to think. In a P-51, the pilot has to open the cockpit and climb out. It is not easy because the plane falls faster and faster, spinning as it goes.

Yeager's heart pounded. He was scared, but he kept his cool. He radioed the other pilots and told them he was in trouble.

> *'I just got hit, and have to bail out.'*
> *— Chuck Yeager*

Yeager was less than five kilometres above the ground and falling fast!

Falling, falling, falling ...

Yeager pulled open the cockpit. A powerful wind hit him in the face as the plane lurched downward. Yeager rolled into the air, and felt the sickening feeling of falling.

He was afraid to open his parachute too soon. It would slow him down, making him an easy target for the German pilots.

As he fell, Yeager ripped off his oxygen mask and helmet, and let them fly away. The rushing air ripped the breath from his lungs. It tore at his eyes and face. His flight suit flapped furiously.

He fell fast, spinning as he went. When Yeager began to feel dizzy, he pulled his ripcord.

Yeager was very glad to see the chute open. It snapped him to an almost a dead stop in midair. The biggest danger had passed. Below him, his plane fell until it crashed to the ground. Yeager was glad he was not in it.

It felt good to drift gently below his parachute. But he was still almost 2500 metres off the ground. Yeager was not safe yet.

An easy target

Yeager searched the ground for a safe place to land. He also searched the sky for his friends. And then he saw the enemy. A German FW-190 circled him and moved in to attack.

Hanging under his parachute, Yeager could do nothing. He slowly floated down, an easy target in the big sky.

Then he saw an American P-51 come in behind the enemy plane. The FW-190 took aim at Yeager and did not watch for other planes. The P-51 shot first, and the German plane exploded.

Yeager guided his parachute to a forest clearing. A small tree appeared in the centre. It snagged his parachute. Thinking fast, Yeager grabbed a branch. He released himself from the parachute, and using the branch, gently lowered himself to the ground.

Saved by the French

Yeager was safely on the ground, but his parachute was still in the tree. It marked his location like a big, white flag. If the enemy found him, they would capture or kill him.

He buried his life jacket and started hiking. Yeager did not know which way to go. He just wanted to get away from the parachute. Before he walked far, a few French people met him.

Yeager spoke no French. The French people spoke no English. They saw his uniform and understood he was American. They wanted to help him.

Danger for everyone

The men took Yeager to an inn. The inn's owner warned him of the real danger. The Germans would kill him, and anyone who helped him, if he were discovered in France.

Yeager had to keep moving. For several days, he sneaked from house to house. Little by little he made his way to Spain. There were no Germans there.

In Spain, Yeager was safe, but he had no way to get home. He was stuck there with five other pilots. The president of Spain would not let them leave until the United States offered them something in return for their pilots.

Finally, the US government sent Spain a shipment of free petrol. Spain sent the United States their six pilots. The boy from West Virginia was finally home.

DATAFILE

TIME LINE ▶▶▶▶

February 1945

> The Cold War begins.

May 1960

> FG Powers is shot down in the
> Soviet Union.

December 1991

> The Cold War ends.

Where is Sverdlovsk?

KEY TERMS ▶▶▶▶

U-2   a special spy plane

telescopic lens
                 a powerful lens for seeing or magnifying the size of a distant object

anti-aircraft missile
                 a missile that can shoot down a plane

CIA   Central Intelligence Agency; the American spy agency

Soviet Union the name given to the country now known as Russia

Chapter Two:
Spy plane shot down

When Francis Gary Powers strapped himself into his U-2 spy plane on 30 April 1960, he thought it would be an easy mission. Powers would fly almost 6000 kilometres over the Soviet Union on the first day of May—a national holiday. His mission: To take pictures of a Soviet missile base for America.

Puppy 68 away!

Powers' codename was 'Puppy 68'. As he took off from a base in Pakistan, a radio message went to Washington, DC. It said, 'Puppy 68 is away!'

What Powers did not know was that a spy saw him take off. The Soviets knew he was coming.

He flew over 24 kilometres high. Because of its long wings, the U-2 could fly higher than any other plane.

At that altitude, the air is very thin. There is very little oxygen. In a U-2, the pilot wears an oxygen mask. He also wears a heavy high altitude flight suit to keep himself warm.

Dragon Lady

The U-2 was a secret aircraft. It had a nickname. It was called 'Dragon Lady'.

Powers liked flying his U-2. It was very quiet at such a high altitude, and very peaceful. He felt safe. No Soviet missiles or fighter jets could reach him—or so he thought. He was speeding along at almost 800 kilometres an hour.

A pilot alone

Powers flew alone. He could not use his radio during the secret mission, so there was no-one to talk to. He also had to breathe through an oxygen mask the whole time.

Powers could see nothing on the ground. It was at least 24 kilometres underneath him! But the camera in the U-2 had a telescopic lens. It could take pictures of trucks, tanks and missiles far below.

Powers thought about his family back in California. They did not know where he was. They did not know he was a spy.

An orange flash

Powers was 2000 kilometres into Soviet territory when he saw a bright orange flash. He did not know what it was. Perhaps it was lightning, he thought. Perhaps it was a flash of the sun.

Powers did not know it, but the Soviets had just shot 14 anti-aircraft missiles at him. One travelled high enough to explode near the U-2. It damaged the plane's tail.

Powers quickly checked his instruments. They did not show any problems. His plane seemed to fly normally. He was still 24 kilometres above the Earth.

But then he felt a change. The plane was sinking. It tipped forward a little, and then a little more.

Big trouble

Powers' heart and brain raced. His instruments showed that he was losing altitude. He tried to raise the U-2's nose. It would not go up. He could not control the plane. He knew he was in trouble—big trouble.

He had to bail out!

The U-2 had one small bomb. But it was not for dropping on an enemy. It was to destroy the plane itself, before it crashed. The CIA did not want the Soviet Union to capture the plane. It was full of secret equipment.

Bailing out

Powers tried to eject out of the cockpit. A small explosion was supposed to throw him and his seat out of the plane.

It was not going to be fun. His plane was falling fast. When he ejected from the cockpit, 600-kilometres-per-hour winds would hit him.

At the same moment, his speed would drop from more than 600 kilometres per hour to almost nothing. The sudden stop would be like hitting a wall.

It could break bones.

Just before he ejected, Powers had to pull his legs out from under the control panel. But they got stuck. If he ejected now, his legs would be torn off.

To get his legs loose, he had to get out of his seat. But then he could not eject. He would have to open the cockpit, crawl out, and jump!

Powers loosened the cockpit roof. The wind ripped it away. A screaming cold wind tore at him. It was hard to move in his heavy flight suit.

He was just about to jump when he remembered the bomb.

Powers had to set off the bomb before he bailed out. He had to destroy the plane in the air. If he did not, the Soviets would find the camera. They would know he was a spy.

Bomb switch

He reached for the switch to set off the bomb. It was a few centimetres too far. Powers tried harder, stretching as far as he could. The wind pulled at him like an angry monster.

Before he could reach the switch, Powers fell from the plane.

His parachute opened at 4500 metres. As Powers drifted almost 5 kilometres to the ground, he saw his U-2 crash and explode below.

Powers landed near some farms in an area called Sverdlovsk, Russia. The people were very surprised. First something exploded nearby. Then a man floated down from the sky.

Powers did not try to escape. He was unarmed and more than 2000 kilometres from any other country. The Soviet police arrested him, but he did not tell them anything about his mission.

The U-2 was not completely destroyed. The Soviets pieced together the wreckage. They found the camera. They knew he was a spy!

Suicide pin

Powers had a suicide pin tipped with poison. If he pricked his skin with it, he would die. It was for an emergency only. If he died, the Soviets could not force him to give them any secret information.

But Powers did not want to die. He had a family. He did not use the pin.

American spy

The Soviet government said that Powers' spy plane proved that the United States was their enemy.

At first, President Eisenhower said that Powers was not a spy. He was only collecting information about the weather. He explained that Powers became lost and strayed into Soviet territory.

But the Soviets had pieces of the U-2. They had the camera. They showed the world that the U-2 was a spy plane. It was embarrassing for the United States.

Prison

The Soviets took Powers to Lubyanka Prison in Moscow, the Soviet capital. They interrogated Powers for 61 days. For 10 to 16 hours a day, they hammered him with questions.

They asked him about his mission, his plane and who sent him. Powers did not tell them any secrets. All he did was apologise.

The Soviets put Powers on trial and found him guilty of spying. Then they sentenced him to three years in prison and seven years of hard labour.

A spy for a spy

In June 1957, the United States had captured Soviet spy Rudolf Abel. The CIA made a deal with the Soviet Union. They would trade a spy for a spy.

Powers came home on 10 February 1962. He never flew another spy mission.

Fifteen years later, Powers' job was to fly a traffic helicopter over Los Angeles. He gave traffic reports.

In 1977, the traffic helicopter crashed. Nobody shot it down. It was caused by a mechanical problem. Francis Gary Powers died in the crash.

Two American spy planes

U-2

Nickname:	Dragon Lady
Wingspan:	32 metres
Length:	19 metres
Height:	4.8 metres
Speed:	764 kilometres per hour
Crew:	One
Maximum Altitude:	21 000+ metres

SR-71

Nickname:	Blackbird
Wingspan:	17 metres
Length:	32.6 metres
Height:	5.5 metres
Speed:	3200 kilometres per hour
Crew:	Two
Maximum Altitude:	
	26 000+ metres

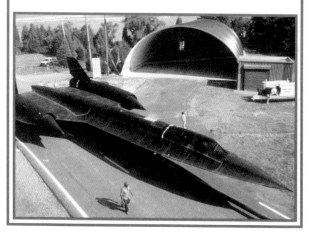

DATAFILE

TIME LINE ▶▶▶▶

May 1981

Pope John Paul II shot and nearly killed.

September 1983

The Soviet Union shoots down a Korean passenger plane.

Where is Sakhalin Island?

KEY TERMS ▶▶▶▶

refuel	to fill a vehicle with more fuel
off course	lost or not flying in the right direction
Su-15	a Soviet Union fighter jet
black boxes	well-protected recording devices used on aircraft to record what happens during a flight
garbled	confused or mixed up

Chapter Three:
Flight 007 shot down

On 1 September 1983, a passenger plane took off from New York City in America to South Korea. The plane was a Korean Airlines Boeing 747. The flight was called Flight 007.

Flight 007 carried 246 passengers and 23 crew members. The plane flew from New York to Alaska. There, it refuelled for the long flight across the Pacific Ocean.

Flight 007 off course

For some reason, Flight 007 went off course. For several hours, Flight 007 flew in the wrong direction. It was still over the Pacific Ocean, but it flew towards the Soviet Union.

No-one noticed that the plane was more than 300 kilometres off course. This was very unusual. Normally, passenger planes are flown very carefully.

On that day, the Soviet Union was testing a new missile. This was during the Cold War. The Soviet Union and the United States were enemies. They did not trust each other. They were both worried about spies and surprise attacks.

The Soviets were worried when their radar showed a plane approaching. It was Flight 007. They thought it was a spy plane. It seemed as if it would fly over their military bases.

Flight 007 moved closer and closer. It was still over the Pacific Ocean, but it was coming closer to the Soviet Union.

Most of the passengers were asleep. They did not expect any problems.

They thought they were flying straight to South Korea.

Soviet fighter planes

As Flight 007 came closer and closer, the Soviets became more and more worried. They did not want an American spy plane over their country.

When the plane did not turn away, the Soviets sent two Su-15 fighter planes to meet it. When the pilots saw it, they knew it was a passenger plane. But was it full of passengers or spy equipment, such as cameras and listening devices?

The cabin lights were out as the passengers slept. The windows were dark.

The Su-15 fighter pilots called to the plane by radio. They told the pilot to turn his plane around. The pilot did not answer.

Flight 007 flew over Sakhalin Island. The island was part of the Soviet Union. It was near the missile test site.

Shoot it down!

The Soviet fighter pilots did not know what to do. They contacted their base. Their commander ordered them to shoot down the 747 if it did not leave Soviet airspace.

The Soviet fighter pilots flew in front of Flight 007. The plane did not turn. Again, they tried to contact Flight 007 by radio. There was no response.

One Su-15 fired cannon shots past Flight 007. It was a warning. The plane did not turn or change its altitude. All it did was slow down. But the pilots on board Flight 007 did not report anything unusual.

Two missiles

Finally, one fighter pilot moved behind the passenger plane. He fired two missiles. Hitting such a large target was an easy shot. The missiles hit the plane. The plane did not explode, but it started to fall.

Out of control and flying in circles, Flight 007 went down. The passengers woke up. They did not know what was happening. They were scared and confused, screaming and holding each other. Some may have put on life jackets and prepared for a crash.

As Flight 007 headed down, the pilots radioed for help. It was the only message that showed there was a problem. They never said anything about seeing the fighter planes.

After 12 terrifying minutes, the plane crashed. It hit the ocean near Sakhalin Island. A Japanese fisherman saw the explosion.

Black boxes

Everyone was killed. But rescuers found only two bodies in the ocean. For six weeks, they looked for the two black boxes. They never found them.

The black boxes were a flight data recorder and a cockpit voice recorder. They contained information about the flight and what the crew said. This information could have answered many questions.

Almost 10 years later, the Soviets gave the US government the missing black boxes. The Soviets had found them and kept them secret. One box was empty. The other box had garbled voice recordings.

Black boxes

After a plane crash, everyone looks for the 'black box'. It is the most important part of the plane. Actually, there are two black boxes aboard passenger planes.

One is a flight data recorder. It records information about the flight. It records direction, altitude, weather, fuel levels and problems with the plane.

The other is the cockpit voice recorder. It records everything the crew says in the cockpit.

If the plane crashes, the information in the black boxes may explain the cause. Investigators need to find them.

What should you do if you find a black box? Do not move it. Do not try to open it. Remember where it is. Call the police.

Unanswered questions

Many people are still asking questions about Flight 007:

- Why did no-one notice that the plane was off course?

- Why did the pilots fail to answer the Soviet radio calls?

- Why did the pilots fail to notice the Soviet fighter planes?

- Why were only two bodies found?

Secret mission?

Some people believe Flight 007 was on a secret mission. Maybe the pilots knew, but the passengers did not know about it.

Today, the Cold War is over. But the true story of Flight 007 is still a mystery.

DATAFILE

TIME LINE ▶▶▶▶

March 2003

> Operation Iraqi Freedom begins.

January 2004

> Captain Kimberly Hampton's helicopter is shot down over Fallujah, Iraq.

Where is Fallujah?

KEY TERMS ▶▶▶▶

invade	to enter an area in order to take it over by force
erupt	to begin violently; to break out
observation helicopter	a helicopter that watches for the enemy
zone	a specific area
attack helicopter	a helicopter that shoots at the enemy
Coalition	a group of countries, or people, who join together to help each other

Chapter Four:
Shot down over Iraq

In January 2004, a battle erupted in the city of Fallujah, Iraq. Iraqi fighters battled coalition forces for the city.

It was a hard battle to fight. The enemy hid in houses and alleys. It was hard to see them. They did not wear uniforms. It was hard to know who was a fighter and who was just a normal person.

The soldiers needed help. They needed to know what was happening—where the enemy was hiding, or where they were shooting.

The military command sent Captain Kimberly Hampton and another American pilot in a Kiowa observation helicopter to fly over the city. Their mission: To spot the enemy and report to the soldiers on the ground. To the coalition soldiers, the Kiowa was like an angel in the sky.

Captain Kimberly Hampton was an excellent pilot. She had flown in battle zones in Afghanistan. She had also flown in South Korea.

Dark Horse Six

Back home in South Carolina, in the USA, Kimberly's friends had always called her 'Kimbo'. She was known for never losing a tennis match.

In Iraq, her helicopter codename was 'Dark Horse Six'. She was known for being smart and brave.

Dark Horse Six flew over the city. Captain Hampton kept the helicopter moving. She did not want to be an easy target. Captain Hampton studied the streets and alleys. When she saw people with weapons, she radioed the troops. Sometimes she called in attack helicopters. They had machine guns, cannons and missiles.

Flying in a war zone is dangerous, but Captain Hampton wanted to help the soldiers on the ground. She did not want the enemy to attack them by surprise.

She kept moving around them, circling and changing altitude. Dark Horse Six was a hard target to hit.

Shot down!

Suddenly a missile shot into the sky. It hit the Kiowa. The helicopter spun down, down, down. It did not explode, but it was out of control. It crashed to the ground near some American troops.

The Americans ran to help. Some helped the pilots while others guarded them against attack.

They could do nothing. Captain Kimberly Hampton was dead.

Three medals

Captain Hampton was the first female American pilot to be killed in Iraq. She was also the first woman from South Carolina to die in Iraq. She was 27 years old when she died.

More than 1200 people went to Kimberly's funeral. They wanted to say goodbye to the hard-working soldier.

Captain Kimberly Hampton won three medals for her courage. At the funeral, the army gave her parents the medals.

The army sent soldiers and a horse to the funeral. It was a black horse with no rider—a horse for Dark Horse Six, Captain Kimberly Hampton.

DATAFILE

TIME LINE ▶▶▶▶

September 2001

Terrorists hijack four passenger planes and crash them into three buildings and a field.

October 2001

The United States and other countries attack terrorist camps in Afghanistan.

Where is Washington DC?

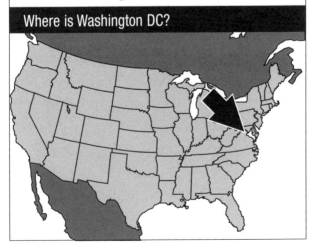

KEY TERMS ▶▶▶▶

hijack — to take over a plane by force

missile — a weapon thrown or projected so that it hits a target at a distance

target — something or someone fired at or marked for attack

air marshal — an armed, undercover officer on a plane

depressurise — to lose pressure

Chapter Five:
Should we shoot down passenger planes?

On 11 September 2001, terrorists hijacked four planes over the United States of America. The terrorists forced their way into the cockpits and took control of the planes.

In the hands of the terrorists, the planes were not just passenger planes. They were missiles—missiles full of people. They carried tonnes of fuel. They could destroy anything they hit.

The terrorists crashed two planes into the World Trade Centre towers in New York. The towers were 110 storeys high.

The planes exploded when they hit. The passengers were killed instantly. Many people in the buildings died in the explosions. Fires trapped other people in the towers.

Firefighters rush in

Hundreds of firefighters rushed into the World Trade Centre towers. They helped thousands of people get out, but they could not put out the fires.

In a short time, the buildings fell. Most people got out, but more than 2700 died.

That morning, the terrorists also flew a plane into the Pentagon in Washington, DC. The Pentagon is the home of the US Department of Defence. More than 180 people died in the plane and the burning building.

The fourth plane

The passengers on the fourth plane heard what was happening in New York and DC. Some of their friends and families called them on mobile phones. They told the passengers about the other planes.

Then the passengers knew what the terrorists were going to do. They knew they were going to die.

Fight for the cockpit

The passengers decided to do something. They had to take control of the plane. Several brave passengers got up and attacked the cockpit.

Nobody knows exactly what happened. There was probably a fight to get into the cockpit. Maybe the pilots died. Maybe passengers and terrorists fought over the controls.

The plane crashed in a field in Pennsylvania. No-one knows why it crashed. Maybe the terrorists made it crash. Maybe the passengers forced it down during the struggle.

After the attacks, many people around the world were afraid of terrorists. No-one knew what to expect. If terrorists hijacked another plane, what would they do with it? What would they hit?

Many targets

There are many targets that could be hit: skyscrapers, government buildings, bridges, military bases, nuclear power plants and sports grounds, just to name a few.

For example, if a plane hit a nuclear power plant, the effect could be terrible. Whole cities would have to be abandoned. Tens of thousands of people might die.

Ready for take-off

Across the world, many countries are now prepared for hijacked planes. If they have to, fighter jets can be sent into the air. They could reach a hijacked plane in only a few minutes.

In some countries the pilots have permission to shoot down planes.

The fighter pilots would do everything possible to avoid shooting down a plane. They'd try to contact the pilots by radio to make sure the plane had been hijacked. They'd fire flares to warn the pilots. They'd fly near the plane and look into the cockpit.

The final order

At some point, the plane may no longer be considered a passenger plane. It could be considered a missile on its way to a target. To save other lives, the fighter pilots may have to shoot it down.

The fighter pilots would probably wait until the last minute. If they cannot force the plane to turn or to land, they may receive a final order to shoot it down.

During the September 11 attacks, US President George W Bush gave the air force a deadly order: Shoot down the hijacked planes heading towards Washington, DC. But the fighter pilots who scrambled to catch the planes never caught their targets.

It was a hard decision to make. Shooting down a passenger plane would kill hundreds of people.

Was it the right decision?

Many people think that President Bush made the right decision to issue this final order on the morning of 11 September 2001. Killing hundreds of people is bad. But letting terrorists kill thousands of people is worse.

Many others think it is wrong to shoot down a passenger plane. They remember the passengers on the plane over Pennsylvania. They think passengers can defend a plane.

'Shoot it down!'

Everyone hopes it is never necessary to shoot down a passenger plane. But someday a fighter pilot might receive the final order: 'Shoot it down'.

- If you were in charge, would you give the order?

- If you were a fighter pilot, would you obey the order?

- If you were a passenger or a pilot, how would you feel about the order?

Officials want to make that decision unnecessary. They want to keep terrorists off planes. Since September 11, many governments have increased airport and aeroplane security.

Checkpoints

For some flights, only passengers with tickets can pass through the security checkpoint. They walk through a metal detector. Sometimes they are also searched. X-ray machines look into suitcases.

Passengers cannot carry things that can be used as weapons. They cannot carry knives, guns, scissors, box cutters, razors or anything that is sharp. They cannot carry liquids that burn, such as petrol.

In spite of the precautions, it is possible that someday terrorists will hijack another plane.

Air marshals

In the United States, some planes have air marshals on board. They would protect the plane if it was hijacked. The air marshals are armed. They are trained for this difficult and dangerous job.

Not all planes have air marshals. Terrorists would never know if there is an air marshal on board. Air marshals wear plain clothes, not uniforms.

Protecting the cockpit

Some pilots think they should be armed. They want to protect the cockpit. But others think pilots should not be armed. Pilots should fly their planes, not fight with terrorists.

A gun on a plane could be very dangerous. At high altitude, a plane is packed with air, like a balloon. Bullet holes might make the plane depressurise. It might even explode. Also, a bullet could easily hit a passenger.

Maybe only air marshals should be armed. But not all planes have air marshals on board. If there is not an air marshal on board, then who is protecting the plane?

The crash sight of Flight 93 in Shanksville, Pennsylvania. The flight, bound for California, was hijacked by terrorists on 11 September 2001.

No-fly zones

Sometimes, planes must stay out of certain areas. These areas are called 'no-fly zones'.

There was a no-fly zone over Washington, DC in June 2004, at the funeral for former US president Ronald Reagan. Many important people were at the funeral, including President Bush, Vice-President Cheney, and the leaders of other countries. During the funeral, no planes could fly nearby.

During terrorism alerts, there are many no-fly zones around major cities and important sites.

Here are some of the rules about no-fly zones:

- Pilots cannot circle or fly close to nuclear power plants.

- Planes must stay away from stadiums during sporting events.

- Planes cannot fly over military bases.

- Planes cannot fly near the White House or the Vice-President's house.

- During meetings of important officials, planes must stay away.

- On New Year's Eve, planes must stay at least eight kilometres from Times Square in New York City.

Book review

Pan Am Flight 103: Terrorism over Lockerbie, by Karen Bornemann Spies. Berkeley Heights, NJ: Enslow Publishers, Inc., 2003.

On 21 December 1988, Pan Am Flight 103 took off from Heathrow Airport in London, England, on its way to JFK Airport in New York, USA. It had 243 passengers and 16 crew members. It never arrived.

Shortly after take-off, the plane disappeared from radar screens. Moments later, something exploded over the village of Lockerbie, Scotland, and a fireball appeared in the sky.

It was Flight 103. Everyone on the plane died. The explosion also killed 11 people in the village.

Pan Am Flight 103: Terrorism over Lockerbie tells the story of this tragic terrorist attack. The book has photos and information about the plane, the passengers and the tragedy in Lockerbie.

Investigators collected every piece of the plane they could find. The police figured out that terrorists had put a bomb in a tape recorder. The tape recorder was in a suitcase. The bomb blew up when the plane reached 9400 metres. A bomb shot down Flight 103.

The book explains how the police figured out who made the bomb. They caught the terrorists and put them on trial in May 2000. Now airline companies are more careful with luggage.

Glossary

air marshal: an armed, undercover officer on a plane

altitude: the vertical position of an object above the sea or land

anti-aircraft missile: a missile that can shoot down a plane

attack helicopter: a helicopter that shoots at the enemy

black boxes: well-protected recording devices used on aeroplanes to record what happens during a flight

CIA: (Central Intelligence Agency) the American spy agency

coalition: a group of countries, or people, who join together to help each other

cockpit: the front of the plane where the pilot sits and controls the plane

depressurise: to lose pressure

elevator: part of the small wing at the back of a plane used to make the plane go up or down

erupt: to begin violently; to break out

garbled: confused or mixed up

hijack: to take over a plane by force

invade: to enter an area in order to take it over by force

missile: a weapon thrown or projected so that it hits a target at a distance

observation helicopter: a helicopter that watches for the enemy

off course: lost or not flying in the right direction

refuel: to fill a vehicle with more fuel

rudder: the part of a plane used to steer it

Soviet Union: the name given to the country now known as Russia

Su-15: a Soviet Union fighter jet

target: something or someone fired at or marked for attack

telescopic lens: a powerful lens for seeing or magnifying the size of a distant object

U-2: a special spy plane

zone: a specific area

Index